PLANETS

SATURN

Alexis Roumanis

LET'S READ
AV2 BY WEIGL
ADDED VALUE · AUDIO VISUAL

www.av2books.com

AV² provides enriched content that supplements and complements this book. Weigl's AV² books strive to create inspired learning and engage young minds in a total learning experience.

Your AV² Media Enhanced books come alive with...

Go to **www.av2books.com**, and enter this book's unique code.

BOOK CODE

Z884593

AV² by Weigl brings you media enhanced books that support active learning.

Audio
Listen to sections of the book read aloud.

Video
Watch informative video clips.

Embedded Weblinks
Gain additional information for research.

Try This!
Complete activities and hands-on experiments.

Key Words
Study vocabulary, and complete a matching word activity.

Quizzes
Test your knowledge.

Slide Show
View images and captions, and prepare a presentation.

... and much, much more!

Published by AV² by Weigl
350 5th Avenue, 59th Floor New York, NY 10118
Websites: www.av2books.com   www.weigl.com

Library of Congress Cataloging-in-Publication Data

Roumanis, Alexis, author.
 Saturn / Alexis Roumanis.
    pages cm. -- (Planets)
 Includes index.
 ISBN 978-1-4896-3300-2 (hard cover : alk. paper) -- ISBN 978-1-4896-3301-9 (soft cover : alk. paper) -- ISBN 978-1-4896-3302-6 (single user ebook)
-- ISBN 978-1-4896-3303-3 (multi-user ebook)
 1. Saturn (Planet)--Juvenile literature. I. Title.
 QB671.R68 2016
 523.46--dc23
                              2014041521

Printed in the United States of America in Brainerd, Minnesota
1 2 3 4 5 6 7 8 9 0 19 18 17 16 15

022015
WEP081214

Project Coordinator: Katie Gillespie Art Director: Terry Paulhus

Weigl acknowledges Getty Images and iStock as the primary image suppliers for this title.

SATURN

CONTENTS

What Is Saturn?

Saturn is a planet. It moves in a path around the Sun. Saturn is the sixth planet from the Sun.

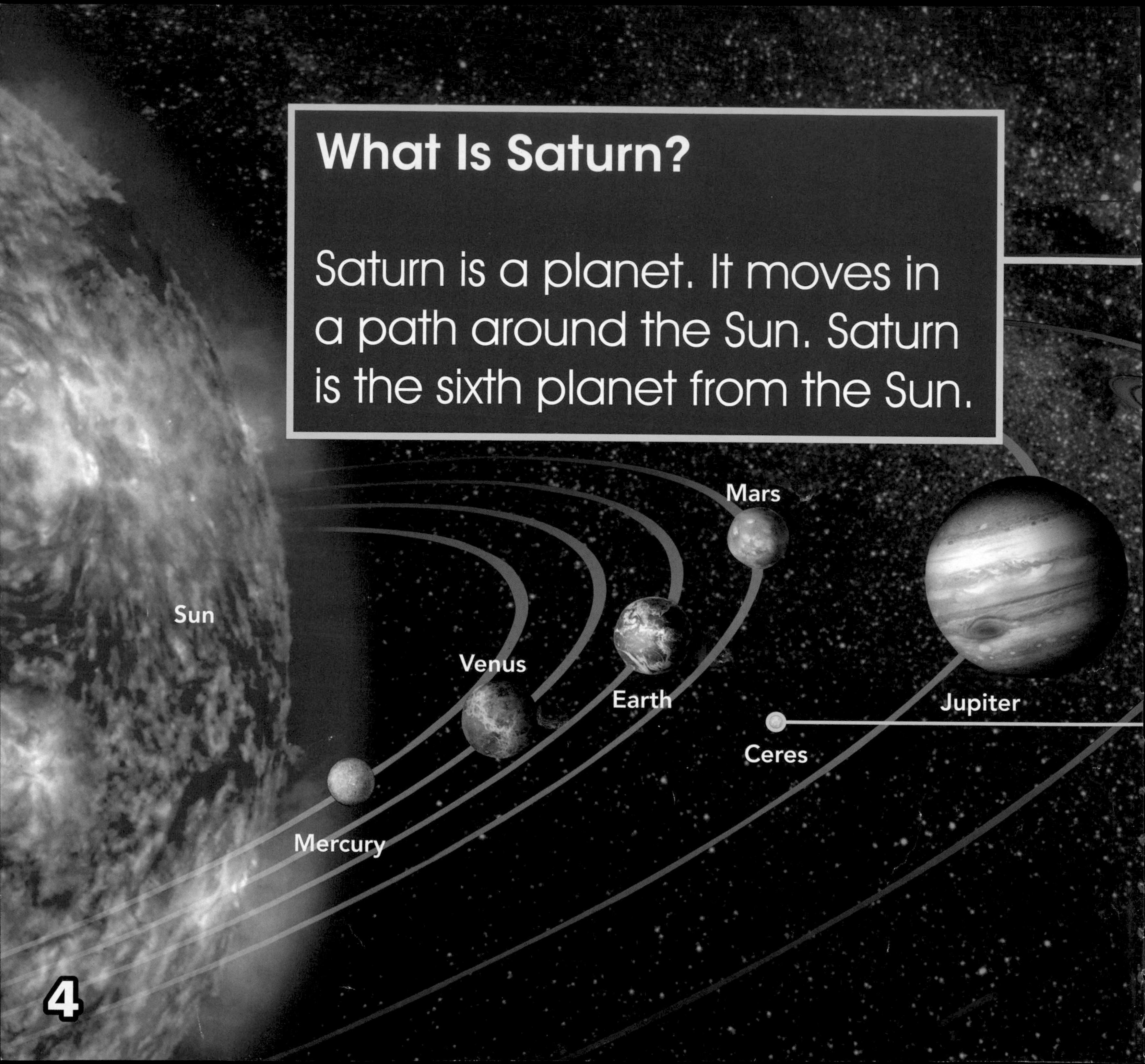

Sun

Mercury

Venus

Earth

Mars

Ceres

Jupiter

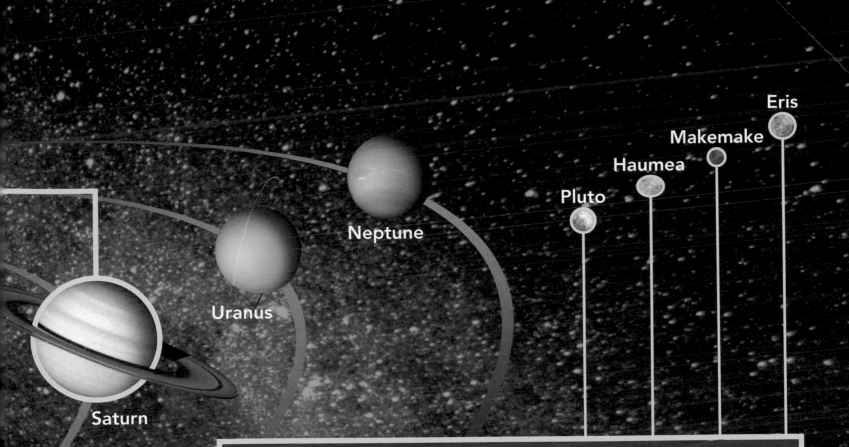

Eris

Makemake

Haumea

Pluto

Neptune

Uranus

Saturn

Dwarf Planets

Dwarf planets are round objects that move around the Sun. Unlike planets, they share their part of space with other objects.

How Big Is Saturn?

Saturn is the second largest planet. It is more than 700 times larger than Earth.

Saturn

Earth

7

What Is Saturn Made Of?

Saturn is a gas giant. It is not made of rock like Earth. Saturn is made up of fast-moving gases.

10

What Does Saturn Look Like?

Saturn looks like it has stripes.
These stripes are gas clouds.
Gas clouds make yellow and
gold lines around the planet.

What Are Saturn's Rings?

Rings make circles around Saturn. They are made of many pieces of rock and ice. There are seven different rings around the planet.

13

Saturn

Titan

What Are Saturn's Moons?

Saturn has 53 known moons. The largest moon is called Titan. Titan is the only known moon to have clouds.

Titan

Who Named Saturn?

Saturn was the farthest planet from the Sun that the Ancient Romans could see. They named the planet Saturn after the god of farming.

17

How Is Saturn Different from Earth?

Saturn is the least solid of the planets. Earth is the most solid planet. Gases make Saturn less solid than Earth.

How Do We Learn about Saturn Today?

Scientists send vehicles called probes into space to study the solar system. A space probe called *Cassini* has been studying Saturn since 2004. It has discovered new moons around the planet.

SATURN FACTS

This page provides more detail about the interesting facts found in the book. They are intended to be used by adults as a learning support to help young readers round out their knowledge of each planet featured in the *Planets* series.

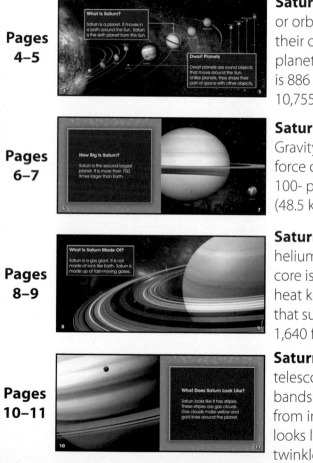

Pages 4–5

Saturn is a planet. Planets are round objects that move around, or orbit, a star, with enough mass to clear smaller objects from their orbit. Earth's solar system has eight planets, five known dwarf planets, and many other space objects that all orbit the Sun. Saturn is 886 million miles (1,427 million kilometers) from the Sun. It takes 10,755 Earth days for Saturn to make one orbit around the Sun.

Pages 6–7

Saturn is the second largest planet. Only Jupiter is bigger. Gravity is a force that pulls objects toward a planet's center. The force of gravity is about the same on Saturn as it is on Earth. A 100- pound (45-kilogram) object on Earth would weigh 107 pounds (48.5 kg) on Saturn.

Pages 8–9

Saturn is a gas giant. Saturn is mostly made up of hydrogen and helium. At the center of the planet is its core. Experts believe that the core is mostly a mixture of water, ice, and rock. Intense pressure and heat keep the core in a solid state. An atmosphere is made of gases that surround a planet. Gases in the atmosphere move at speeds of 1,640 feet (500 meters) per second.

Pages 10–11

Saturn looks like it has stripes. When viewed through a telescope, Saturn appears to have yellow and gold bands. These bands are gas clouds, caused by Saturn's fast winds, and heat rising from inside the planet. Saturn is also very bright. From Earth, Saturn looks like a yellowish star. Unlike a star, Saturn does not appear to twinkle, as planets shine with a steady light.

Pages 12–13

Rings make circles around Saturn. Saturn is not the only planet with rings. Jupiter, Uranus, and Neptune also have rings. Saturn's rings are the largest and easiest to see. The rock and ice in the rings range in size. Some are tiny pieces of dust. Others are mountain-sized boulders. Experts believe Saturn's rings are asteroids and comets that broke into small pieces before they reached the planet.

Pages 14–15

Saturn has 53 known moons. Astronomers have discovered nine provisional moons around Saturn. Together, Saturn and its moons are called the Saturnian System. Titan is the second largest moon in the solar system. Its atmosphere is similar to what Earth's atmosphere was probably like before life began to develop. Titan's atmosphere is about 95 percent nitrogen, with traces of methane.

Pages 16–17

Saturn was the farthest planet from the Sun that the Ancient Romans could see. It also had the slowest orbit of all the planets that they could see. In addition to the planet, the Ancient Romans also named a day of the week after the god, Saturn. The word "Saturday" comes from the phrase *dies Saturni*, meaning "Saturn's Day."

Pages 18–19

Saturn is the least solid of the planets. Saturn is much larger than Earth. About 764 Earth-sized planets could fit inside Saturn. Although Saturn is the larger planet, it is mostly made of gases, while Earth is mostly made of rock. Gases are less dense than rock. For this reason, Earth is about eight times as dense as Saturn.

Pages 20–21

Scientists send vehicles called probes into space to study the solar system. *Cassini* has been used to find several moons since it arrived near Saturn. In 2005, it discovered a moon called Daphnis inside Saturn's rings. *Cassini* has also been used to find rivers and lakes of methane on Titan's surface. *Cassini* carried a smaller space probe to Titan called *Huygens*, which landed on Titan in 2005. *Huygens* sent back pictures of Titan's surface to Earth.

KEY WORDS

Research has shown that as much as 65 percent of all written material published in English is made up of 300 words. These 300 words cannot be taught using pictures or learned by sounding them out. They must be recognized by sight. This book contains 54 common sight words to help young readers improve their reading fluency and comprehension. This book also teaches young readers several important content words. These words are paired with pictures to aid in learning and improve understanding.

Page	Sight Words First Appearance
4	a, around, from, in, is, it, moves, the, what
5	are, of, other, part, that, their, they, with
6	big, Earth, how, more, second, than, times
8	like, made, not, up
11	and, does, has, lines, look, make, these
12	different, many, there
15	have, only
16	after, could, see, was, who
19	most
21	about, been, do, learn, new, study, to, we

Page	Content Words First Appearance
4	path, planet, Saturn, Sun
5	dwarf planets, objects, space
8	gases, gas giant, rock
11	clouds, stripes
12	circles, ice, pieces, rings
15	moons, Titan
16	Ancient Romans, farming, god
21	*Cassini*, probes, scientists, solar system